MW00593572

America's Christian Heritage

By
Paul K. Blair

April 2008
Second Printing

Direct Inquiries To:

Paul K. Blair
1230 North Sooner Road
Edmond, Oklahoma 73034
E-Mail: pblair@fairviewbaptistedmond.org

ISBN 978-1-60643-258-7

Table of Contents

Chapter 1
Introduction

The children of Israel had wandered
in the wilderness for forty years as the
generation brought out of Egypt died
in the wilderness because of their lack
of faith in Almighty God. As their
children were preparing to cross the
Jordan River and enter into the land
that God had promised to give them,
God reminded that next generation of
the covenant that He had made with
them. They were reminded of who
their God was.

*"Hear, O Israel: The LORD our God
is one LORD: And thou shalt love the
LORD thy God with all thine heart,
and with all thy soul, and with all thy
might. And these words, which I
command thee this day, shall be in
thine heart: And thou shalt teach
them diligently unto thy children, and
shalt talk of them when thou sittest in*

*thine house, and when thou walkest
by the way, and when thou liest down,
and when thou risest up.''
(Deuteronomy 6:4-7)*KJV

They were given a solemn warning
that once they were established in the
land and things were going well and
they felt secure and the economy was
good - DO NOT FORGET THE
LORD who has blessed you and
delivered you.

Deuteronomy 6:10-12
*"When the LORD thy God shall have
brought thee into the land which he
sware unto thy fathers, to Abraham,
to Isaac, and to Jacob, to give thee
great and goodly cities, which thou
buildedst not, And houses full of all
good things, which thou filledst not,
and wells digged, which thou diggedst
not, vineyards and olive trees, which
thou plantedst not; when thou shalt
have eaten and be full; Then beware*

lest thou forget the LORD, which brought thee forth out of the land of Egypt, from the house of bondage."

Deuteronomy 8:7-11
For the LORD thy God bringeth thee into a good land, a land of brooks of water, of fountains and depths that spring out of valleys and hills; A land of wheat, and barley, and vines, and fig trees, and pomegranates; a land of oil olive, and honey; A land wherein thou shalt eat bread without scarceness, thou shalt not lack any thing in it; a land whose stones are iron, and out of whose hills thou mayest dig brass. When thou hast eaten and art full, then thou shalt bless the LORD thy God for the good land which he hath given thee. Beware that thou forget not the LORD thy God, in not keeping his commandments, and his judgments, and his statutes, which I command thee this day:

3

Deuteronomy 8:17-20

And thou say in thine heart, My power and the might of mine hand hath gotten me this wealth. But thou shalt remember the LORD thy God: for it is he that giveth thee power to get wealth, that he may establish his covenant which he sware unto thy fathers, as it is this day. And it shall be, if thou do at all forget the LORD thy God, and walk after other gods, and serve them, and worship them, I testify against you this day that ye shall surely perish. As the nations which the LORD destroyeth before your face, so shall ye perish; because ye would not be obedient unto the voice of the LORD your God.

God even gave them reminders to direct their focus back to Him so that they would always remember who they were in relationship to Him and that He was their Sovereign God. The actual Passover was a one-time event. However, the Jews were instructed to celebrate this day annually as *"a memorial"* (Exodus 12:14) to remember the Lord who was their Redeemer.

The tassels in their prayer shawls were designed specifically with the number of strings and knots to remind them of God and His Law with each glance,. *"That ye may remember, and do all my commandments and be holy unto your God."* (Numbers 15:40)

After crossing the Jordan River the Jews were instructed to take twelve stones out of the middle of the riverbed and place them as a memorial marker, *"...and these stones shall be for a memorial unto the children of Israel forever."* (Joshua 4:7)

Their key to success as a nation was to remember that Jehovah was their God and they were his people.

To summarize, God was saying, "Don't forget who I am, don't forget who you are, and don't forget where you came from. If you do, you'll forget who is in charge and you'll lose your way."

This is certainly a truth known and exploited by the secularists. Karl Marx, the father of modern Communism, is credited to have said, *"A people without a heritage are easily persuaded."*

Woodrow Wilson issued a prophetic and ominous warning in a speech made in 1911:

"A nation which does not remember what it was yesterday, does not know what it is today, nor what it is trying to do. We are trying to do a futile thing if we do not know where we came from or what we have been about...The Bible...is the one supreme

*source of revelation of the meaning
of life, the nature of God and spiritual
nature and needs of men. It is the only
guide of life which really leads the
spirit in the way of peace and
salvation. America was born a
Christian nation. America was born
to exemplify that devotion to the
elements of righteousness which are
derived from the revelations of Holy
Scripture."*

Even with all these warnings, we have
lost our way in America. We have
had our heritage stolen by groups like
the ACLU and other secular humanist
movements. We are now being told
that God has no place in America.
We are told that America was purely
a secular nation founded by Atheists
and Deists who were products of
enlightenment thinking. We brag that
our success as a nation is due to our
own intellect and ingenuity. We have
forgotten God.

In early 2007, I was with a group of preachers and their wives being led by the brilliant historian, David Barton, on a tour of the United States Capitol. While standing in the Rotunda, Mr. Barton held up a  book that is now being used in many of our major public universities entitled, *The Godless Constitution.* He turned to the back page, normally reserved for a bibliography. But in this case, there was only a blank page instead of references and a note stating that the authors chose not to use the "scholarly apparatus" of using footnotes and including a bibliography. In other words, they were saying that we have no references to support our message, but you can trust us. After all, we are university professors.

Barton then began to read to us from original documents proving the great faith of our founders and the influence that God and the Holy Scriptures had in the establishment of this great nation.

Here we were standing in the Capitol Rotunda, having just passed by the statue of John Peter Gabriel Muhlenberg. In January, 1776, Pastor Muhlenberg preached a message in his church from Ecclesiastes, Chapter 3. After completing his message, he descended from his pulpit and took off his clerical robes   revealing the uniform of a colonial army officer. Then he said something to the effect that "there is a time to pray and there is a time to fight, and that time is now." Then he led some three hundred

men from his congregation to join General George Washington and the Continental Army. Pastor Muhlenberg rose to the rank of Major General before the war ended.

In the Capitol Rotunda itself stands another statue of an influential preacher in America's history, James A. Garfield, the 20th President of the United States. David Barton read from an original letter written by Garfield recounting his preaching revivals and seeing people saved.

Dear Bro. Wallace,
We have just closed our meeting with happy results. There were 34 additions; 31 by immersion. I was sorry I could not be in Newburgh last Sunday, but in seemed to be my duty to stay here. Bro. Dave Shu tells me that the Brethren want me to hold a meeting in vacation. I have spoken 19 discourses in our meeting here - and

*this with all our work in the school
has worn me down very much. I
would not think of holding a meeting
alone. And don't know as I ought to
help hold one. I will be in your place
sometime next week and talk with you
in reference to the matter of your
letter. Which would have been
answered sooner but for the meeting.
I shall hope to visit Bedford also.*

*Love to your family & believe me
your brother,*
J. A. Garfield
Encircling the Rotunda, are eight
beautiful paintings, each 12 feet tall

and 18 feet wide, documenting great moments of America's history. Of these, four were very religious in nature. Paintings depicting the Baptism of Pocahontas by John Gadsby Chapman and also the departure of the Pilgrims by Robert W. Weir. Clearly seen in the picture of the Pilgrims are John Robinson, William Bradford, William Brewster and the others praying and reading the Holy Bible which is clearly opened to the introductory page of the New Testament.

How surreal. We see firsthand an undocumented college text book professing that our founding fathers were Atheists and Deists. Yet here we were standing in the middle of the US Capitol seeing statues dedicated to great preachers, seeing pictures depicting the Christian influence on our nation, and reading original documents that bear irrefutable evidence that 238 of the 250 men that we would call our Founding Fathers were in fact traditional, fundamental Christians.

Chapter 2
The Twisted Interpretation of the First Amendment

After the reformation, Europe eventually settled into a religious system of state churches. In order to get along one needed to be a member of the **state sanctioned denomination** or risk persecution.   For instance, Germany was Lutheran; Switzerland was Calvinist; Scotland was Presbyterian; England was Anglican; France was Roman Catholic, etc. The Pilgrims, having separated from the Church of England rather than face continued persecution, fled to America for Christian liberty.

Their Mayflower Compact states: *"...Having undertaken for the Glory of God, and Advancement of the Christian Faith, and the Honour of our King and Country, a voyage to plant the first colony in the northern*

parts of Virginia... "
Over the following decades, tens of thousands came from Europe to America for religious liberty.

Consider this excerpt from the Constitution of the New England Confederation, May 19, 1643:

"Whereas we all came to these parts of America with the same end and aim, namely to advance the kingdom of our Lord Jesus Christ and to enjoy the liberties of the Gospel thereof with purities and peace, and for preserving and propagating the truth and liberties of the gospel... "

Unfortunately, over time America became very similar to what they left in Europe, as different states had denominational ties. Massachusetts was Puritan, Pennsylvania was Quaker, Rhode Island was Baptist, Connecticut was Congregationalist, etc. In order to get along in most states you needed to be a part of that state's denomination.

Then, the "Great Awakening" took place. As ministers like Jonathon Edwards and George Whitefield preached with conviction, tens of thousands realized that salvation was not the result of denominational membership, but of a genuine act of repentance and commitment of faith in the finished work of Jesus Christ. True Christianity was not in joining a particular sect but by being "born again".

One of Whitefield's illustrations used when preaching to a crowd of thousands while standing on the steps of the Courthouse in Boston follows:

"Father Abraham, whom have you in heaven? Any Episcopalians? No! Any Presbyterians? No! Have you any

Independents or Seceders? No! Have you any Methodists? No! No! No! Whom have you there? We don't know those names here! All who are here are Christians."

Rev. George Whitfield

The colonists began "tolerating" one another. They may have had minor differences in doctrinal beliefs, but they were unified by their faith in One God, manifest as Father, Son, and Holy Ghost, and by their belief in the Scriptures of the Old and New Testament as the perfect, inerrant Word of God.

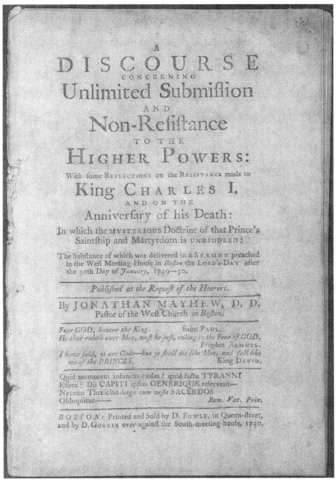

Published sermon by Rev. Jonathon Mayhew, 1749-1750 (Library of Congress)

This revival in America, called the Great Awakening, was the primary factor that compelled the colonies to unity and liberty.

John Adams credited patriot pastors as being *"the most conspicuous, the most ardent and influential in the awakening of the revival of American principles and feelings."*

Although the humanists insist that Christianity has no part in America's founding, the facts prove otherwise. On September 7, 1774, at the first meeting of the Continental Congress at Carpenter's Hall in Philadelphia, the Reverend Jacob Duche' was asked to come and open the session that day in prayer. The group read from the 35th Psalm and prayed for three hours.   John Adams wrote his wife about the significance of this day:

" I never saw a greater effect upon an audience. It seems as if heaven had ordained that Psalm to be read on that morning. After this, Mr. Duche', unexpectedly to every body, struck out into an extemporary prayer, which

filled the bosom of every man present. I must confess, I never heard a better prayer, on one so well pronounced."

This three-hour prayer meeting and Bible study should raise an obvious question. Why would a group of Atheists and Deists spend three hours praying to a God that they didn't believe existed (Atheism) or cared (Deism) and why would they read a book that neither believed was the Word of God? Atheists and Deists wouldn't, but Orthodox Christians would.

Chapter 3
The Faith of our Founding Fathers

Patricia Banomi, Professor Emeritus of New York University, in an article entitled *The Middle Colonies as the Birthplace of American Religious Pluralism,* stated: *"The colonists were about 98 percent Protestant."* Research by historian David Barton agrees, stating that 98.4 percent were Protestant Christian, 1.4 percent were Catholic and .2 percent were other, mostly Jewish.

Let us examine briefly the lives and faith of some of the most famous of our Founding Fathers.

George Washington

Among George Washington's many well known accolades are these:

- He was a delegate from Virginia to the First and Second Continental Congress, 1774-1775.

- He was the Commander in Chief of the Continental Army during the Revolutionary War, 1775-83

- He was the President of the Constitutional Convention, where the United States Constitution was formulated, May 14, 1787 - September 17, 1787.

- He was the First President of the United States of America, 1789-97.

These facts you probably already knew, but the following testimonies about George Washington you probably didn't know.

As a young man, George Washington kept a prayer journal that he titled *"Daily Sacrifice."* Consider some of the entries:

"O God, who is rich in mercy and plenteous in redemption, mark not, I beseech Thee, what I have done amiss; remember that I am but dust, and remit my transgressions, negligences and ignorances, and cover them all with the obedience of Thy dear Son, that those sacrifices (of

sin, praise and thanksgiving which I have offered may be accepted by Thee, in and for the sacrifice of Jesus Christ offered upon the Cross for me."

On another day, he recorded:

"Direct my thoughts, words and work wash away my sins in the immaculate Blood of the Lamb, and purge my heart by Thy Holy Spirit...daily frame me more and more into the likeness of Thy Son Jesus Christ."

 These quotations don't sound like a Deist, but they do certainly sound fitting for a man who has been repeatedly remembered in paintings as a man of prayer. Even in the United States Capitol today there is a private prayer room only accessible by members of Congress. In the front of that room is a beautiful piece of stained glass artwork forever memorializing General Washington on his knees in prayer.

One of his first directives as the Commander in Chief of the Continental Army reads as follows:

"The General most earnestly requires and expects a due observance of those articles of war established for the government of the army, which forbid profane cursing, swearing, and drunkenness. And in like manner he requires and expects of all officers and soldiers, not engaging in actual duty, a punctual attendance on Divine service, to implore the blessing of Heaven upon the means used for our safety and defense."

Why would an Atheist or Deist require regular church attendance? Or care about drunkenness and cursing? These sound more like the actions of a Christian.

On the following pages are copies of excerpts from a conduct Manual for the United States Navy. These copies were obtained through the Library of Congress. Notice the requirements to attend church twice on Sundays

RULES for the regulation of the Navy of the United Colonies.

THE Commanders of all ships and vessels belonging to the Thirteen United Colonies, are strictly required to shew in themselves a good example of honour and virtue to their officers and men, and to be very vigilant in inspecting the behaviour of all such as are under them, and to discountenance and suppress all dissolute, immoral and disorderly practices, and also such as are contrary to the rules of discipline and obedience, and to correct those who are guilty of the same, according to the usage of the sea.

THE Commanders of the ships of the Thirteen United Colonies are to take care, that divine service be performed twice a day on board, and a sermon preached on Sundays, unless bad weather or other extraordinary accident prevents.

IF any shall be heard to swear, curse or blaspheme the name of God, the Commander is strictly enjoined to punish them for every offence, by causing them to wear
a wooden

a wooden collar, or some other shameful badge of distinction, for so long time as he shall judge proper. If he be a com-missioned officer, he shall forfeit one shilling for each offence, and a warrant or inferior officer, six-pence. He who is guilty of drunkenness, if a seaman, shall be put in irons, until he is sober, but if an officer he shall forfeit two days pay.

No Commander shall inflict any punishment upon a seaman beyond twelve lashes upon his bare back with a cat of nine tails; if the fault shall deserve a greater punishment, he is to apply to the Commander in Chief of the navy, in order to the trying of him by a Court-Martial, and in the mean time he may put him under confinement.

The Commander is never by his own authority to discharge a Commission or Warrant officer, nor to punish or strike him; but he may suspend or confine them, and when he comes in the way of a Commander in Chief apply to him for holding a Court-Martial.

The officer who commands by accident of the Captain, or Commander's

C   absence

unless there were extraordinary circumstances which prohibited attendance.

On May 12, 1779, General George Washington was visited at his Middle Brook military encampment by the Chiefs of the Delaware Indian tribe. They brought three youths to be trained in the American schools. Washington assured them:

"You do well to wish to learn our arts and ways of life, and above all, the religion of Jesus Christ. These will make you a greater and happier people than you are. Congress will do everything they can to assist you in this wise intention; and to tie the knot of friendship and union so fast, that nothing shall ever be able to loose it....And I pray God He may make your Nation wise and strong."

Does this sound like the ramblings of a Deist? *"You do well to learn...above all, the religion of Jesus Christ.*" Does Washington sound like an advocate for the separation of church and state as he assured the chiefs that *"Congress will do everything they can"* to see this happens.

It was George Washington who chose to take his oath of office as our first President with his hand resting on the Holy Bible, and this is still the custom to this day.

George Washington's inauguration included a two-hour worship service at St. Paul's Cathedral immediately after he was sworn in to office.

President Washington said in his inaugural address, *"the propitious smiles of Heaven can never be expected on a nation that disregards the eternal rules of order and right which Heaven itself has ordained."*

Was George Washington an Atheist or Deist? No. The evidence is overwhelming that George Washington was faithful to his orthodox Christian beliefs.

John Adams

John Adams was a member of the First and Second Continental Congresses in 1774 and 1775. He served as the U.S. Minister to France in 1783. Along with John Jay and Benjamin Franklin, he signed the Treaty of Paris, officially ending the Revolutionary War. Afterwards, he served as the U.S. Minister to Great Britain from 1784 to 1788, then became the Vice-President under George Washington from 1789 to 1797. Finally, Adams was elected the second President of the United States, serving from 1797-1801. He was the first president to live in the White House.

On February 22, 1756, as a young man of only 20, John Adams made the entry in his diary, his idea of a "Eutopian Nation"(sic):

"Suppose a nation in some distant Region should take the Bible for their only law Book, and every member should regulate his conduct by the precepts there exhibited! Every member would be obliged in conscience, to temperance, frugality, and industry; to justice, kindness, and charity towards his fellow men; and to piety, love, and reverence toward

Almighty God...What a Eutopia, what a Paradise would this region be(sic)."

This certainly does not sound like a dream of an Atheist or a Deist.

Recognizing the vital role that Christianity played in the well being of a nation that was rooted in personal liberty, President Adams wrote on October 11, 1798:

"We have no government armed with power capable of contending with human passions unbridled by morality and religion. Avarice, ambition, revenge, or gallantry, would break the strongest cords of our Constitution as a whale goes through a net. Our Constitution was made only for a moral and religious people. It is wholly inadequate to the government of any other."

Finally, in a letter written to Thomas

Jefferson on June 28, 1813, John Adams, remembering the motivation for Independence and the glue that held America together, wrote:

"The general principles, on which the Fathers achieved independence, were the only Principles in which that beautiful Assembly of young Gentlemen could Unite....And what were these general Principles? I answer, the general Principles of Christianity, in which all these Sects (denominations) *were United: And the general Principles of English and American Liberty, in which all those young Men United, and which had United all Parties in America, in Majorities sufficient to assert and maintain her Independence.*

Now I will avow, that I then believe, and now believe, that those general Principles of Christianity, are as eternal and immutable, as the

*Existence and Attributes of God; and
that those Principles of Liberty, are as
unalterable as human Nature and our
terrestrial, mundane System."*

Samuel Adams

Sam Adams was the cousin of John
Adams and was known as "Father of
the American Revolution." He
created the *Committees of
Correspondence* in 1772, in order to
have trusted communication up and
down the East Coast. Adams also
instigated the Boston Tea Party,
signed the Declaration of

Independence, called for the first Continental Congress, and served as a member of Congress until 1781. He labored over 20 years as a patriot and leader. The night of Paul Revere's midnight ride, the British were marching to Lexington to capture Sam Adams and John Hancock, who happened to be staying at the home of Jonas Clark, the pastor of the church in Lexington. The State of Massachusetts, as evidence of the high esteem in which he was held, chose to be represented by a statue of Samuel Adams in the U.S. Capitol.

What about the faith of this man who played such a vital role in America's independence? Was this "Father of the American Revolution" an Atheist or a Deist? In an excerpt from an article Samuel Adams wrote on November 20, 1772, entitled, *"The Rights of the Colonist as Christians,"* he declared:

"The right to freedom being the gift of God Almighty, the rights of the Colonists as Christians may best be understood by reading and carefully studying the institutions of The Great Law Giver and the Head of the Christian Church, which are to be found clearly written and promulgated in the New Testament."

This fine Christian, Sam Adams, believed that our rights were a gift from God, and they were outlined in the New Testament. In fact, it was Representative Sam Adams who on September 6, 1774, the second day of the first meeting of the Continental Congress, proposed that the session be opened with prayer.

On October 4, 1790, Samuel Adams wrote the following letter to his cousin, John Adams, who was then the Vice-President of the United States:

"Let divines and philosophers, statesmen and patriots, unite their endeavors to renovate the age, by impressing the minds of men with the importance of educating their little boys and girls, of inculcating in the minds of youth the fear and love of the Deity and universal philanthropy, and, in subordination to these great principles, the love of their country; of instructing them in the art of   self -government without which they never can act a wise part in the   govern- ment of societies, great or small; in short, of leading them in the study and practice of the exalted   virtues of the Christian system."

Finally, Sam Adams wrote the following testimony in his Last Will and Testament :

"Principally, and first of all, I resign my soul to the Almighty Being who gave it, and my body I commit to the

dust, relying on the merits of Jesus Christ for the pardon of my sins"

Atheist or Deist? Hardly!!

Patrick Henry

Patrick Henry was an American Revolutionary leader and gifted orator. While debating before the Virginia Provincial Convention meeting in the House of Burgesses on March 23, 1775, he spoke this famous phrase, *"Is life so dear or peace so sweet as to be purchased at the price of chains and slavery? Forbid it,*

41

Almighty God! I know not what course others may take; but as for me, give me Liberty or give me death!"

Henry was Commander-in-Chief of the Virginia Militia, a member of the Virginia General Assembly and House of Burgesses, 1765; and a member of the Continental Congress, 1774-75. He was a five-time Governor of the State of Virginia and was instrumental in writing the Constitution of Virginia. Patrick Henry was offered numerous positions by President George Washington and Congress, including: Secretary of State, Chief Justice of the Supreme Court, U.S. Minister to Spain, and U.S. Minister to France; but he declined them all.

Patrick Henry once stated:

"Bad men cannot make good citizens. It is impossible that a nation of infidels or idolaters should be a

nation of free-men. It is when a people forget God, that tyrants forge their chains. A vitiated state of morals, a corrupted public conscience, is incompatible with freedom."

He is also credited to have said:

"It cannot be emphasized too strongly or too often that this great nation was founded, not by religionists, but by Christians; not on religions, but on the Gospel of Jesus Christ."

In 1784, Patrick Henry supported a Bill establishing a "Provision for Teachers of the Christian Religion" stating:

"The general diffusion of Christian knowledge hath a natural tendency to correct the morals of men, restrain their vices, and preserve the peace of society..."

Patrick Henry, once interrupted while engaged in Bible reading, held up his Bible and said:

"The Bible is worth all other books which have ever been printed, and it has been my misfortune that I have never found time to read it with the proper attention and feeling till lately. I trust in the mercy of Heaven that it is not yet too late."

Shortly before his death, in a letter to Archibald Blair, January 8, 1799, Patrick Henry commented on the French Revolution:

"And, whilst I see the dangers that threaten ours from her [France's] intrigues and her arms, I am not so much alarmed as at the apprehension of her destroying the great pillars of all government and of social life, - I mean virtue, morality, and religion. This is the armor, my friend, and this

alone, that renders us invincible. These are the tactics we should study. If we lose these, we are conquered, fallen indeed."

On November 20, 1798, in his Last Will and Testament, Patrick Henry wrote:

"I have now disposed of all my property to my family; there is one thing more I wish I could give them, and that is the Christian religion. If they had that, and I had not given them one shilling, they would be rich, and if they had not that, and I had given them all the world, they would be poor. This is all the inheritance I give to my dear family. The religion of Christ will give them one which will make them rich indeed."

What a beautiful testimony from a wonderful Christian husband, father and American Statesman.

John Jay

John Jay was appointed by President
George Washington as the First Chief
Justice of the U.S. Supreme Court.
Jay was a member of the First and
Second Continental Congresses and
served as the President of the
Continental Congress. In 1777, John
Jay helped to write the Constitution
of New York, and he served as
Governor of the State of New York
from 1795 to 1801.

In addition to his civic duties, John
Jay was elected president of the

Westchester Bible Society in 1818 and president of the American Bible Society in 1821. On May 13, 1824, while serving as its president, John Jay gave an address to the American Bible Society:

"By conveying the Bible to people thus circumstanced, we certainly do them a most interesting kindness. We thereby enable them to learn that man was originally created and placed in a state of happiness, but, becoming disobedient, was subjected to the degradation and evils which he and his posterity have since experienced. The Bible will also inform them that our gracious Creator has provided for us a Redeemer, in whom all the nations of the earth shall be blessed; that this Redeemer has made atonement "for the sins of the whole world," and thereby reconciling the Divine justice with the Divine mercy has opened a way for our redemption

and salvation; and that these inestimable benefits are of the free gift and grace of God, not of our deserving, nor in our power to deserve."

On October 12, 1816, John Jay admonished:

"Providence has given to our people the choice of their rulers, and it is the duty, as well as the privilege and interest of our Christian nation to select and prefer Christians for their rulers."

On May 17, 1829, John Jay was drawing near death after a life of serving his country. As recorded by his son, Judge William Jay, John Jay was asked if he had any words for his children, to which he responded:

"They have the Book!"

Dr. Benjamin Rush

Dr. Benjamin Rush was a patriot, doctor, educator and philanthropist. He served as a member of the Continental Congress, 1776-77, and was a signer of the Declaration of Independence. In 1774, he helped found and was president of the Pennsylvania Society for Promoting the Abolition of Slavery. He also helped found and served as Vice-President of the Philadelphia Bible Society. Rush was a principal promoter of the American Sunday School Union; and a member of the Abolition Society. He also served as the Surgeon General of the

Continental Army, 1777-78, helped to write the Pennsylvania Constitution and served as Treasurer of the U.S. Mint from 1797 to 1813.

In his work, *A Plan for Free Schools*, 1787, Dr. Benjamin Rush counseled:

"Let the children...be carefully instructed in the principles and obligations of the Christian religion. This is the most essential part of education."

On July 13, 1789, in a letter to Jeremy Belknap, Dr. Benjamin Rush stated:

"The great enemy of the salvation of man, in my opinion, never invented a more effectual means of extirpating Christianity from the world than by persuading mankind that it was improper to read the Bible at schools."

In his work titled *Essays, Literary, Moral, and Philosophical*, Dr. Benjamin Rush explained:

"Christianity is the only true and perfect religion, and that in proportion as mankind adopts its principles and obeys its precepts, they will be wise and happy. In contemplating the political institutions of the United States, I lament that we waste so much time and money in punishing crimes and take so little pains to prevent them. We profess to be republicans, and yet we neglect the only means of establishing and perpetuating our republican forms of government, that is, the universal education of our youth in the principles of Christianity by the means of the Bible. For this Divine book, above all others, favors that equality among mankind, that respect for just laws, and those sober and frugal virtues, which constitute

the soul of republicanism."

Dr. Benjamin Rush was certainly one of the most outspoken and influential Christian patriots.

Charles Carroll

Charles Carroll is probably most well known by most Americans by the portrayal of him in the opening scenes of the fiction thriller *National Treasure.* But Carroll was an ardent patriot and Christian.

Born in Annapolis, Maryland, Carroll became one of the richest men in the Colonies, yet risked it all for the cause of liberty. Charles Carroll was a member of the Continental Congress, one of the first to sign the Declaration of Independence, and was the oldest surviving member of the signers, dying in 1832 at the ripe old age of 95.

On November 4, 1800, in a letter to James McHenry, Charles Carroll, wrote about the vital relationship between Christian morality and the health of our free government:

"Without morals a republic cannot subsist any length of time; they therefore who are decrying the Christian religion, whose morality is so sublime and pure [and] which insures to the good eternal happiness, are undermining the solid foundation of morals, the best security for the

duration of free governments."

In a letter to the Rev. John Stanford on October 9, 1827, Carroll explained his reasoning for entering into the struggle for independence:
"To obtain religious as well as civil liberty I entered jealously into the Revolution, and observing the Christian religion divided into many sects, I founded the hope that no one would be so predominant as to become the religion of the State. That hope was thus early entertained, because all of them joined in the same cause, with few exceptions of individuals."

Carroll shared his beautiful Christian testimony on September 27, 1825, in a letter to Charles W. Wharton, Esq.:

"On the mercy of my Redeemer I rely for salvation and on His merits not on the works I have done in obedience to

His precepts."

Hardly the words of an Atheist or a Deist. The truth is the overwhelming majority of the Colonists were Christians. Historian David Barton states that of the 250 men that could be considered our Founding Fathers, 238 held orthodox, Christian beliefs.

Yet, whom do the revisionist historians talk about all the time? Usually they refer to the least religious of our founders -- Benjamin Franklin and Thomas Jefferson. Yet even those testimonies are greatly exaggerated. Although they were considered the least religious of our founders, they still knew far more Bible than most fundamental Christians of our day, and they held to a Biblical World View.

During the Convention to write the Constitution in 1787, disagreements between the large and small states and between the northern and southern states were about to stop the progress of the entire Constitutional process. Then the elder statesman, Benjamin Franklin delivered this most famous oration:

Mr. President:

The small progress we have made after 4 or 5 weeks close attendance & continual reasonings with each other - our different sentiments on almost every question, several of the last producing as many noes as ayes, is methinks a melancholy proof of the imperfection of the Human Understanding.

We indeed seem to feel our own want of political wisdom, since we have been running about in search of it. We have gone back to ancient history for models of Government, and examined the different forms of those Republics which, having been formed with the seeds of their own dissolution, now no longer exist. And we have viewed Modern States all round Europe, but find none of their Constitutions suitable to our circumstances.

In this situation of this Assembly, groping as it were in the dark to find political truth, and scarce able to distinguish it when presented to us, how has it happened, Sir, that we have not hitherto once thought of humbly applying to the Father of lights to illuminate our understanding?

In the beginning of the Contest with G. Britain, when we were sensible of danger, we had daily prayer in this room for Divine protection. - Our prayers, Sir, were heard, & they were graciously answered. All of us who were engaged in the struggle must have observed frequent instances of a

Superintending Providence in our favor.

To that kind Providence we owe this happy opportunity of consulting in peace on the means of establishing our future national felicity. And have we now forgotten that powerful Friend? or do we imagine we no longer need His assistance?

I have lived, Sir, a long time, and the longer I live, the more convincing proofs I see of this truth - that God Governs in the affairs of men. And if a sparrow cannot fall to the ground without His notice, is it probable that an empire can rise without His aid? We have been assured, Sir, in the Sacred Writings, that "except the Lord build the House, they labor in vain that build it." I firmly believe this; and I also believe that without his concurring aid we shall succeed in this political building no better than

*the Builders of Babel: We shall be
divided by our partial local interests;
our projects will be confounded, and
we ourselves shall become a reproach
and bye word down to future ages.
And what is worse, mankind may
hereafter from this unfortunate
instance, despair of establishing
Governments by Human wisdom and
leave it to chance, war and conquest.*

*I therefore beg leave to move - that
henceforth prayers imploring the
assistance of Heaven, and its blessing
on our deliberations, be held in this
Assembly every morning before we
proceed to business, and that one or
more of the clergy of this city be
requested to officiate in that service.*

Franklin, the man called irreligious by
the revisionists, was the man behind
prayer in Congress!!

In fact, the Library of Congress has in

its records the first draft of the proposed Seal for the new United States Government. It shows Moses and the Israelites on one side, a cloud and a pillar of fire in the middle, and the Egyptians drowning in the Red Sea on the other side, a direct reference to the biblical account recorded in the Book of Exodus. Around the outside were the words *"Rebellion to tyrants is obedience to God.."*

Whose right-wing, radical idea was this? Which religious zealots proposed this? Benjamin Franklin and Thomas Jefferson.

Men like Franklin and Jefferson were the least religious of our Founding Fathers, but that is a relative comparison. They were not men void of faith and when compared to modern standards they would be recognized as men with a great

knowledge of the Bible and reverence
for the Holy Scriptures.

Proposed Seal for the United States
On July 4, 1776, Congress appointed Benjamin Franklin, Thomas Jefferson
and John Adams "to bring in a device for a seal for the United States of
America."

Chapter 4
The Declaration

Knowing that King George III, had placed himself above the Law of God and above English Law as established by the Magna Carta, the American Colonists followed English Law for the removal of a tyrannical government. As the Declaration of Independence was signed, Sam Adams said, *"We have this day restored the Sovereign to Whom all men ought to be obedient. He reigns in heaven and from the rising to the setting of the sun, let His kingdom come."*

Fifty-six patriots representing thirteen individual colonies gathered in Philadelphia to covenant themselves together in the establishment of a new sovereign nation called the United States of America.

This document clearly states the basis for this new Nation.

*"When in the Course of human events it becomes necessary for one people to dissolve the political bands which have connected them with another and to assume among the powers of the earth, the separate and equal station **to which the Laws of Nature and of Nature's God** entitle them, a decent respect to the opinions of mankind requires that they should declare the causes which impel them to the separation.*

*We hold these truths to be self-evident, that all men are **created equal**, that **they are endowed by their Creator with certain unalienable Rights,** that among these are Life, Liberty and the pursuit of Happiness. **That to secure these rights, Governments are instituted among Men**."*

We in the 21st Century read phrases like *"pursuit of happiness"* or the *"Laws of Nature and Nature's God."* and suppose that the authors were just writing in some 18th Century prose. The truth is that they were using clearly defined legal terms and were speaking very directly.

Sir William Blackstone was a scholar and lawyer whose *Commentaries on Law* were considered the cornerstone of English Law in the 18th Century. To become a lawyer in this era, one had to study extensively Blackstone's

Commentaries and also the Holy Bible. After all, how could one practice the Law without knowing *the Law*?

The *Blackstone Commentaries on Law, Book One, Section Two*, reads as follows:

"Man, considered as a creature, must necessarily be subject to the laws of his Creator, for he is entirely a dependent being ... And consequently, as man depends absolutely upon his Maker for everything, it is necessary that he should in all points conform to his Maker's will. <u>This will of his Maker is called the law of nature...</u> And if our reason were always, as in our first ancestor (Adam) *before his transgression, clear and perfect, unruffled by passions, unclouded by prejudice, unimpaired by disease or intemperance, the task would be pleasant and easy; we should need no*

*other guide but this. But every man
now finds the contrary in his own
experience; that his reason is corrupt,
and his understanding full of
ignorance and error. This has given
manifold occasion for the benign
interposition of divine providence;
which, in compassion to the frailty,
the imperfection, and the blindness of
human reason, hath been pleased, at
sundry times and in divers manners,
to discover and enforce it's laws by an
immediate and direct revelation. The
doctrines thus delivered we call the
<u>revealed or divine law, and they are to
be found only in the holy scriptures.</u>
...Upon these two foundations, the
law of nature and the law of
revelation, depend all human laws;
that is to say, no human laws should
be suffered to contradict these."*

The will of our Maker is defined as
the *"law of nature"* and it has been
revealed to man in the Holy

Scriptures.

In other words, the United States of America was established on the Laws of God as recorded for us in the Holy Scriptures. That is the Foundation of America. And the opening paragraphs of the Declaration of Independence clearly state that our Creator God alone grants rights, and the purpose of government is to secure these rights to man.

But what about the phrase *"Pursuit of Happiness"?* Certainly that must mean we have the right to do whatever we want in order to be happy. Right? WRONG.

Blackstone's Commentaries on Law, Book 2, Chapter 1, states as follows:

For he has so intimately connected, so inseparably interwoven <u>the laws of eternal justice with the happiness of</u>

each individual, that the latter cannot be attained but by observing the former; and, if the former be punctually obeyed, it cannot but induce the latter. In consequence of which mutual connection of justice and human felicity (happiness), he has not perplexed the law of nature with a multitude of abstracted rules and precepts, referring merely to the fitness or unfitness of things, as some have vainly surmised; but has graciously reduced the rule of obedience to this one paternal precept, "that man should pursue his own true and substantial happiness." This is the foundation of what we call ethics, or natural law.

Man as a creation can only be happy when he is in the will of his Creator. Therefore the Government cannot interfere with a man's quest to obey and walk in the will and laws of God as defined in the "Laws of Nature and

Nature's God" which we have already
seen speak of the Holy Bible.

Chapter Five
The Constitution

The Declaration of Independence was our original governing document and we mark the birth of our country from the day of its signing. The Constitution was added eleven years later, *"In order to form a more perfect Union."* In the Declaration of Independence, our founders clearly stated their beliefs. God gives rights to man and the government's role is to protect those God-given rights. Those rights are enumerated in the *"laws of nature and nature's God.."* According to Book One, Section Two of Blackstone's Commentaries on Law (which was THE AUTHORITY on English Law for several hundred years and where this phrase comes from) the phrase *"laws of nature and nature's God"* mean the laws of God for his creation as revealed in the Holy Scriptures.

The Constitution itself was a mutual covenant agreement binding together these thirteen sovereign colonies and clearly defining the roles and the limits of the Federal Government.

America was not designed to be a Theocracy and would not be called a *"Christian Nation"* for that reason. But as we have already seen, America was predominantly populated by orthodox Christian people, and our form of government was based on the laws and principals found in the Holy Bible.

The **First Amendment** protected the American Citizen's rights to *"preach the Gospel"* (Mark 16:15) and *"not to forsake the assembling of yourselves together."* (Hebrews 10:25) Therefore, those God-given rights of peaceable assembly, freedom of worship, freedom of speech, and freedom of the press were granted.

The **Second Amendment,** which grants the right to keep and bear arms, is protected by Luke 11:21, where Jesus said, *"When a strong man armed keepeth his palace, his goods are in peace."*

The **Fourth Amendment** that protects a person's property from unreasonable search and seizure is referenced in Deuteronomy 24:10-11: *"When thou dost lend thy brother any thing, thou shalt not go into his house to fetch his pledge. Thou shalt stand abroad, and the man to whom thou dost lend shall bring out the pledge abroad unto thee."*

The **Eighth Amendment** that protects from "cruel and unusual punishment" is a scriptural mandate where the punishment is to fit the crime. *(Eye for eye, tooth for tooth).*

Our three **branches of government** are patterned after the three positional offices of Christ as found in Isaiah 33:22: *"For the LORD is our judge, the LORD is our lawgiver, the LORD is our king; he will save us."* (Judicial, Legislative, Executive)

Our Republican form of government is found in Deuteronomy 1:15: *"So I took the chief of your tribes, wise men, and known, and made them heads over you, captains over thousands, and captains over hundreds, and captains over fifties, and captains over tens, and officers among your tribes."*

Equal representation by state is found in Numbers 1:4-5: *"And with you there shall be a man of every tribe; every one head of the house of his fathers. And these are the names of the men that shall stand with you."*

The **Uniform Immigration Laws** of Article 1, Section 8 come from Leviticus 19:34: *"But the stranger that dwelleth with you shall be unto you as one born among you, and thou shalt love him as thyself; for ye were strangers in the land of Egypt: I am the LORD your God."*

The requirement that the **President must be a natural born citizen** being taken from Deuteronomy 17:15: *"Thou shalt in any wise set him king over thee, whom the LORD thy God shall choose: one from among thy brethren shalt thou set king over thee: thou mayest not set a stranger over thee, which is not thy brother."*

Article 3, Section 3 pertaining to **witnesses in a trial** is from Deuteronomy 17:6: *"At the mouth of two witnesses, or three witnesses, shall he that is worthy of death be put to death; but at the mouth of one witness he shall not be put to death."*

Provisions against attainder come from Ezek 18:20: *"The soul that sinneth, it shall die. The son shall not bear the iniquity of the father, neither shall the father bear the iniquity of the son: the righteousness of the* *righteous shall be upon him, and the wickedness of the wicked shall be upon him.."*

Churches being exempt from taxation comes from Ezra 7:24: *"Also we certify you, that touching any of the priests and Levites, singers, porters, Nethinims, or ministers of this house of God, it shall not be lawful to impose toll, tribute, or custom, upon them."*

The most famous of the Amendments from which the falsely applied **"Separation of Church and State"** has been derived is the First, which states: *"Congress shall make no law respecting an establishment of religion, or prohibiting the free exercise thereof; or abridging the freedom of speech, or of the press; or the right of the people peaceably to assemble, and to petition the Government for a redress of* *grievances."*

At the time of the signing of the Declaration of Independence, at least nine states had state-sanctioned denominations. At the time of the signing of the Constitution, six states still had state-sanctioned denominations.

The purpose of the First Amendment was to prohibit the Federal Government from establishing a national denomination or interfering with other already established Christian denominations. In other words, the Federal government was to keep its nose out of the business of state governments.

With that being understood, were the state governments supposed to be secular, religious-free zones? You be the judge.

Consider the Constitution of

Delaware (1776): *ARTICLE 22: Every person who shall be chosen a member of either house, or appointed to any office of place of trust, before taking his seat or entering upon the execution of his office, shall...make and subscribe the following declaration, to wit: "I, _____, do profess faith in God the Father, and in Jesus Christ His only Son, and in the Holy Ghost, one God, Blessed forevermore; and I do acknowledge the Holy Scriptures of the Old and New Testament to be given by Divine inspiration."*

Also, consider the Constitution of Pennsylvania (1776): Section 10: *And each member, before he takes his seat shall make and subscribe the following declaration, viz: "I do believe in one God, the Creator and Governor of the Universe, the Rewarder of the good and Punisher* *of the wicked. And I do acknowledge the Scriptures of the Old and New Testament to be given by Divine Inspiration. And <u>no further or other religious test</u> shall ever hereafter be required of any civil officer of magistrate in this State.*

The citizens of the state of Pennsylvania said the only requirement for public service was that you had to believe in the one true Triune God and believe that the Bible is His Holy Word. <u>Other than that,</u> there is no test and the Federal government was prohibited from expanding or taking away from that.

Our founders realized that this great American experiment where individuals had so much personal liberty must also be tied to personal responsibility.

Since they were trying to limit the external constraints typical of a tyrannical government, it was absolutely necessary that each individual be capable of self restraint. That was to be accomplished through the belief in an absolute all-knowing, all-seeing, all-powerful, perfect Sovereign God and adhering to His will as given in the Holy Scriptures.

Chapter 6
God and Education

In 1962, in the Court *Case Engel v. Vitale*, the United States Supreme Court decided that this voluntary prayer offered every day at the beginning of the school day was "un-Constitutional":

"Almighty God, we acknowledge our dependence upon Thee, and we beg thy blessings upon us, our parents, our teachers and our Country."

Then in the 1963 case *School District of Abington Township v. Schempp*, the United States Supreme Court decided that opening the school day with the reading of a few Bible verses could be *"psychologically harmful to the child."*

Again in 1980, the Supreme Court ruled in the case *Stone v. Graham*, that copies of the Ten Commandments could not be posted in public schools because *"if the posted copies of the Ten Commandments are to have any effect at all, it will be to induce the schoolchildren to read, meditate upon, perhaps to venerate and obey the Commandments...this is not permissible...under the establishment clause."*

What a dangerous thing to risk teaching a student. Things like don't kill, don't steal, don't lie, and don't commit adultery. With each passing school year we see a number of cases where the ACLU seeks to prohibit seniors from praying at their graduation and from making any reference in their graduation speeches to faith in God or Jesus Christ.

When something is declared "unconstitutional" it means our Founding Fathers would have

84

disapproved of it.

Well what did our Founders intend?

Tens of thousands of Puritans migrated to New England within twenty years of the Mayflower's landing at Plymouth. The first public school act in America was implemented by them in 1647: It reads:

"To the end that learning may not be buried in the graves of our forefathers...every township, after the Lord hath increased them to the number of fifty householders, shall appoint one to teach all children to read and write; and where any town shall increase to the number of one hundred families, they shall set up a grammar school, the masters thereof being able to instruct youth so far as they may be fitted for the university."

This was called the *"Old Deluder Act"*, because it was intended to defeat Satan, the Old Deluder, who had used illiteracy in the Old World to keep people from reading the Word of God. In other words, the main purpose of schools in Puritan New England was to teach children to read the Bible.

In 1787, during the same meeting where Congress drafted the Constitution, they also drafted the *Northwest Ordinance* outlining the governing of new territories north and west of the Ohio River. In this ordinance Congress clearly stated the function of education in Article 3:

"...religion, morality, and knowledge, being necessary to good government and the happiness of mankind, schools and the means of education shall forever be encouraged."

Religion, morality and knowledge!! President George Washington, in his farewell address spoke of the importance of religion and morality to the future well being of America:

"Of all the dispositions and habits which lead to political prosperity, religion and morality are indispensable supports. In vain would that man claim the tribute of patriotism, who should labor to subvert these great pillars of human happiness...And let us with caution indulge the supposition that morality can be maintained without religion."

America's future stood on two pillars: religion and morality. Of course, as we have seen in previous chapters, the term religion was synonymous with Christianity or Christian denomination. President Washington said that we would be foolish to suppose that we could continue to be a moral people without being a religious people.

In fact, Noah Webster, who compiled the Webster's Dictionary and wrote the first public school history book in 1835, entitled *"Republican Government"* said this:

"It is the sincere desire of the writer that our citizens should early understand that the genuine source of correct republican principles is the Bible, particularly the New Testament or the Christian Religion."

In his work, *A Plan for Free Schools*, 1787, Dr. Benjamin Rush counseled: *"Let the children...be carefully instructed in the principles and obligations of the Christian religion. This is the most essential part of education."*

Charles Carroll wrote in 1800:

"Without morals a republic cannot subsist any length of time; they therefore who are decrying the Christian religion, whose morality is so sublime and pure [and] which insures to the good eternal happiness, are undermining the solid foundation of morals, the best security for the duration of free governments."

Universities were established on the same foundation.

Harvard - Founded in 1636 and named for the Puritan Reverend John Harvard for the purpose of training ministers of the Gospel.

"Let every student be plainly instructed and earnestly pressed to consider well the main end of his life and studies is to know God and Jesus

Christ which is eternal life (John 17:3) " - **Laws and Statutes for Students, 1643**

Yale - Formed in 1701 and named for Elihu Yale, a wealthy Puritan.

"All scholars shall live religious, godly, and blameless lives according to the rules of God's Word, diligently reading the Holy Scriptures, the fountain of Light and truth; and constantly attend upon all the duties of religion, both in public and secret." – **New Charter, 1745**

William and Mary. Named for the popular British monarchs who in 1688 established the supremacy of Parliamentary rule over the monarchy.

"There are three things which the Founders of this College proposed to themselves, to which all its Statutes

should be directed.

The first is that the youth of Virginia should be well educated to learning and good morals.

The second is that the churches of America, especially Virginia, should be supplied with good ministers after the doctrine and government of the Church of England, and that the college should be a constant seminary for this purpose.

The third is that the Indians of America should be instructed in the Christian religion, and that some of the Indian youth that are well behaved and well inclined, being first well prepared in the Divinity School, may be sent out to preach the gospel to their countrymen in their own tongue, after they have duly been put in orders of deacons and priests." –

The Statutes of William and Mary, 1727 Columbia - Founded in 1754 and called King's College, was renamed in 1784.

"The chief thing that is aimed at in this college is to teach and engage children to know God in Jesus Christ."

Princeton - Founded in 1746 and whose Presidents included the Rev. John Witherspoon and the Rev. Jonathon Edwards.

"Cursed be all that learning that is contrary to the cross of Christ" – Rev. Jonathan Dickinson, First President of Princeton.

One hundred four of the first 119 colleges and universities in America were founded by Christians. Of the first 40,000 college graduates in

America before the Civil War, 10,000 entered into the ministry.

Abraham Lincoln once said that *"the philosophy of the classroom in one generation becomes the philosophy of government in the next."*

It is for that reason the teaching of the Bible was so important. Religion was the key to morality, and morality was the key to the continuance of this Republic called the United States of America

As President John Adams said, *"We have no government armed with power capable of contending with human passions unbridled by morality and religion. Avarice, ambition, revenge, or gallantry, would break the strongest cords of our Constitution as a whale goes through a net. Our Constitution was made only for a moral and religious people. It is wholly inadequate to the government of any other."*

Our founding fathers knew what they were talking about. Every measure of morality in America whether it be murder, theft, violence, sexual immorality, abortion, divorce, alcoholism, drug abuse, etc., remained constant from 1900 to 1960. Even during the Great Depression there was no spike in crime.

But since that first ruling in 1962, all these measurements of moral decay have skyrocketed. If only we had listened and heeded the wise counsel of the Father of our Nation, *"And let us with caution indulge the supposition that morality can be maintained without religion."*

America: One Nation Under God

The Nazi Minister of Propaganda, Joseph Goebbels, operated under the belief that if you tell a lie long enough and loud enough and outrageous enough and no one refutes it, then it will become accepted as fact.

It is ironic that those who profess to be defenders of civil liberty are actually the ones responsible for stripping us of our liberty. Think about the fact that we have more laws on the books now than ever before in the history of the world, yet there has never been a time of such lawlessness in our society. Now we have strip searches at the airports, metal detectors at the entrances of many public schools and camera-bag and purse searches at any sporting event. Are we really a freer people now that we are not "restrained" by the Bible?

Unfortunately, Christians in America have been told about the fabled *"separation of church and state"* for so long that we have believed it and acted accordingly. We have abandoned the public square, and secularism has been glad to fill that void.

Our Founding Fathers knew that Christianity could not be forced upon any man. When one is confronted with his own sinfulness, presented with the Good News of the Gospel of Jesus Christ, convicted by the drawing and convincing of the Holy Spirit, that person has the choice either to believe or not to believe. That is an action of his own will.

America is not and was never intended to be a "theocracy." Christianity is not compulsory. However, our nation was founded on basic Biblical principles, and any who wish to live in America as citizens must be willing to honor and adhere to the Law of the Land. America was founded on the laws and precepts given to us in the Holy Bible.

Consider these court decisions:

In 1799, Runkel v. Winemiller:
"By our form of government, the Christian religion is the established religion; and all sects and denominations of Christians are placed upon the same equal footing."

In 1838, Commonwealth v. Abner Kneeland: *"The First Amendment embraces all who believe in the existence of God, as well...as Christians of every denomination... This provision does not extend to atheists, because they do not believe in God or religion; and therefore... their sentiments and professions, whatever they may be, cannot be called religious sentiments and professions."*

In **1846, City of Charleston v. S.A. Benjamin,** in maintaining that a secular store should be closed on Sunday – *"Christianity is a part of the common law of the land"*

In the 1892, Supreme Court Case, the Church of the Holy Trinity v. the United States: *"We are a religious people....this is a Christian Nation."*
Consider also the actions of our

Continental Congress on September 11, 1777. While General Washington was suffering a defeat nearby, Congress instructed its Committees of Commerce to import 20,000 Bibles *"from Scotland, Holland or elsewhere"* because the Bible was of such great importance to the future well-being of America.

Philadelphia was about to fall to the British; yet instead of packing their belongings and getting out of town, Congress was talking about the need to import 20,000 Bibles. Isn't that a strange thing for a group of "atheists and deists" to be concerned with? Wouldn't that be considered a clear violation of "the separation of church and state" by today's standards? Isn't that showing preference of one belief system over the other?

We have been conned for long enough. It is time for Christians to come out of hiding and become the "Salt and Light" that Jesus commanded us to be.

Chapter 8
Reclaiming America
One State at a Time

In my lifetime, we have gone from *Andy Griffith* to *Desperate Housewives.* We have gone from *Rio Bravo* to *Brokeback Mountain.* We have gone from teachers having to concern themselves with children bringing concealed gum to school to being concerned over bringing concealed weapons to school.

Who is going to stand for
righteousness in America?

The only answer is for men and
women of God to stand up and be Salt
and Light as our Lord Jesus Christ
commanded us to be. There is no
place in the Bible where we are told
to sit and wait, but we are told to
occupy until He comes again.

After all, it is our calling. God
charged the prophet Ezekiel in
Chapter 33:7-9:

*"O son of man, I have set thee a
watchman unto the house of Israel;
therefore thou shalt hear the word at
my mouth, and warn them from me.*

*When I say unto the wicked, O wicked
man, thou shalt surely die; if thou
dost not speak to warn the wicked
from his way, that wicked man shall
die in his iniquity; but his blood will I*

require at thine hand..

Nevertheless, if thou warn the wicked of his way to turn from it; if he do not turn from his way, he shall die in his iniquity; but thou hast delivered thy soul."

After the first sin in Genesis 3, we see the very first prophet of God in Genesis 4 contending for his culture and preaching, *"Behold, the Lord cometh with ten thousands of his saints, To execute judgment upon all, and to convince all that are ungodly among them of all their ungodly deeds which they have ungodly committed, and of all their hard speeches which ungodly sinners have spoken against him."* (Jude 14-15)

Enoch, Moses, Jonah, Samuel, Elijah, Nathan, Isaiah, Ezekiel, Daniel, Jeremiah, John the Baptist, etc. - all preached repentance not only to the

103

common man but also to those in authority.

"When the righteous are in authority, the people rejoice: but when the wicked beareth rule, the people mourn." (Proverbs 29:2) was true then and it still is today.

Pastors in America, as we have seen, played prominent roles in America's founding and continued growth. We have had pastors sign the Declaration of Independence, serve in the Senate and House of Representatives, serve as Speaker of the House, serve as Major Generals and even serve as the President.

Presbyterian, Baptist and Congregational Pastors of the mid -1700's became known as the *"Black Regiment"* by the British Parliament as they would ascend their pulpits every Sunday and stir the people's hearts with dreams of liberty and righteousness.

Pastors served in or led local militias of Minute Men, as they would preach on Sunday morning then drill after lunch.

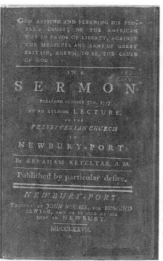 As we have seen and heard testimony from our Founding Fathers themselves that the Great Awakening was the single event most responsible for the Declaration of Independence.

The Library of Congress bears record of Election Sermons as the local church played a key role in local and national elections. Only since 1954, when then-Senator Lyndon

Johnson tacked on an eleventh-hour amendment to a tax bill which slipped through without debate and threatened the tax-exempt status of churches that got too involved in American Republicanism, did Christians begin to sound the retreat.

Consider this timeline: In 1954 churches began to grow silent; by 1963 the Bible and prayer were removed from public schools; by 1965 the sexual revolution was in full force; by 1973 the Supreme Court found a solution for all the unwanted consequences of the sexual revolution as Roe v. Wade was handed down, and by 1980 the Ten Commandments were removed from the public square. Since then we have seen the continued teaching of Atheism (evolution).

We are no longer taught that we are fearfully and wonderfully made by a loving Creator God for a divine purpose; we are instead the accidental products of the random evolutionary process with no purpose in life except to get all we can and live for ourselves. It's no wonder that we have seen the explosion of teenage suicides and school shootings over the last generation.

I see today an America very similar to the one that existed in 1729. Plenty of churches, plenty of people going through the motions, but very little Spirit-filled Christianity.

Just as a great revival swept the pulpits of America then, the same can happen today.

First, we must realize that true Christianity is not just a compartment of our lives. It is not just an attitude that we put on Sunday mornings, then take off to live life. Our Founding

Fathers had a true Biblical World View. They looked at every situation in this life through the lens of Scripture and sought God's counsel on every subject. We must do the same. If Jesus Christ is truly our Lord, then He is the Lord of ALL and not just the Lord of Sunday morning.

The second thing we must do is invoke God's conditional promise for restoration of a backslidden people -- repentance and prayer.

"If I shut up heaven that there be no rain, or if I command the locusts to devour the land, or if I send pestilence among my people; If my people, which are called by my name, shall humble themselves, and pray, and seek my face, and turn from their wicked ways; then will I hear from heaven, and will forgive their sin, and will heal their land." **2 Chronicles 7:13-14**

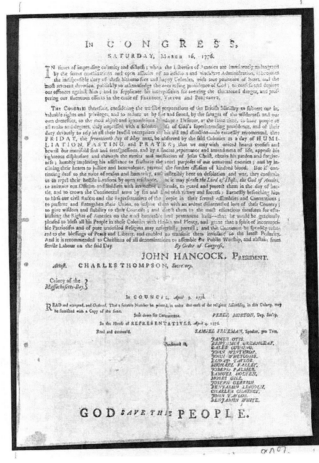

Copy of a call to humbling, prayer and fasting
by the Continental Congress on March 16,
1776. Basically this document is invoking
God's conditional promise of 2 Chronicles
7:14. (from Library of Congress)

Christians must repent and turn to God and seek His face with petitions of prayer. There is not much difference in the lifestyle of most professing Christians and non-Christians these days. If we truly believed in the things we claim to believe, would we really live the way we live? Christians must examine themselves whether they be in the faith (2 Corinthians 13:5), turn from their own wicked ways, and plead for a genuine revival in the land.

Our nation has claimed this verse in more dire times than these and God has been faithful. On the preceding page is a copy of an original call by the Continental Congress to invoke the promises of 2 Chronicles 7:14 just four months prior to the signing of the Declaration of Independence.

Immediately following is the transcript from a call to humility, repentance and prayer issued by President Abraham Lincoln during the darkest days of the Civil War.

By the President of the United States of America. A Proclamation:

Whereas, the Senate of the United States, devoutly recognizing the Supreme Authority and just Government of Almighty God, in all the affairs of men and of nations, has, by a resolution, requested the President to designate and set apart a day for National prayer and humiliation.

And whereas it is the duty of nations as well as of men, to own their dependence upon the overruling power of God, to confess their sins and transgressions, in humble sorrow, yet with assured hope that genuine repentance will lead to mercy and pardon; and to recognize the sublime truth, announced in the Holy Scriptures and proven by all history, that those nations only are blessed whose God is the Lord.

And, insomuch as we know that, by His divine law, nations like individuals are subjected to punishments and chastisements in this world, may we not justly fear that the awful calamity of civil war, which now desolates the land, may be but a punishment, inflicted upon us, for our presumptuous sins, to the needful end of our national reformation as a whole People? We have been the recipients of the choicest bounties of Heaven. We have been preserved, these many years, in peace and prosperity. We have grown in numbers, wealth and power, as no other nation has ever grown.

But we have forgotten God. We have forgotten the gracious hand which preserved us in peace, and multiplied and enriched and strengthened us; and we have vainly imagined, in the deceitfulness of our hearts, that all these blessings were produced by some superior wisdom and virtue of our own.

Intoxicated with unbroken success, we have become too self-sufficient to feel the necessity of redeeming and preserving grace, too proud to pray to the God that made us!

It behooves us then, to humble ourselves before the offended Power, to confess our national sins, and to pray for clemency and forgiveness. Now, therefore, in compliance with the request, and fully concurring in the views of the Senate, I do, by this my proclamation, designate and set apart Thursday, the 30th. day of April, 1863, as a day of national humiliation, fasting and prayer. And I do hereby request all the People to abstain, on that day, from their ordinary secular pursuits, and to unite, at their several places of public worship and their respective homes, in keeping the day holy to the Lord, and devoted to the humble discharge of the religious duties proper to that solemn occasion. All this being done, in sincerity and truth, let us then rest humbly in the hope authorized by the Divine teachings, that the united cry of the Nation will be heard on high, and answered with blessings, no less than the pardon of our national sins, and the restoration of our now divided and suffering Country, to its former happy condition of unity and peace.

Abraham Lincoln
March 30, 1863

Notice how President Lincoln calls to record the sins warned of in

Deuteronomy 8:11-20 and the remedy
required in 2 Chronicles 7:14.

God has answered this prayer before.
Is He not capable of doing so again?

The third thing we must do is
evangelize (be Light).

The great theologian from the 20th
Century, Francis Scheaffer, stated that
the best way to contend for the culture
is to win people to Christ. To that we
say AMEN!! We are to be reaching
the unsaved with the blessed Gospel
and then discipling them to Christian
maturity.

But we have abandoned evangelism.
We no longer go out to reach the lost
world. Instead we have gone into the
entertainment business and tried to
attract them to church. Quite frankly,
a church that preaches the whole
counsel of God without compromise

will never be attractive to the lost world. Rather than reaching the masses, today's churches in America are successfully taking members away from each other.

The Bible's methods always work. Consider the exploits of the Apostle Paul as recorded in the Book of Acts. He preached publicly and from house to house. What were the results? Some believed, some didn't believe, and usually a riot broke out. Should we think that the results today will be much different? We must preach the truth in love and we must equip our people to be evangelists who are comfortable and capable with sharing the Gospel of Jesus Christ with others.

There are many great programs including *Evangelism Explosion* and *Sharing Jesus without Fear* that are effective tools to be used by churches.

When churches decide to get out of the entertainment business and start going out and preaching Jesus, as Paul did, we will see the beginnings of revival.

The fourth thing we must do is educate our children.

Abraham Lincoln once said that *"the philosophy of the classroom in one generation becomes the philosophy of government in the next."*

Unfortunately, the institution of public education that was founded on *"religion, morality and knowledge"* is now compelled by the Federal government to teach Atheism and call it Science.

When I was in the fourth grade, the father of one of my classmates (a Methodist preacher) came to our class in December to teach us the

Christmas Story and gave every child a New Testament. Now, both he and the teacher would be arrested for compromising the "separation of church and state."

Take an active role in your local school board meetings. Be involved in the selection process of your school's curriculum. Check out the textbooks your child brings home and be aware of what is being taught. Meet with your child's teacher and learn about his/her goals for education and subjects to be discussed. Investigate the type of books in the school library. If you aren't satisfied, run for a seat on the School Board yourself or help recruit someone from your church that could help in maintaining or improving the quality of education being provided at the local level.

If you aren't satisfied with public education then investigate local private Christian schools or consider home schooling. There are great home school support networks to assist you so you aren't going it alone. Talk to your pastor. Perhaps your church could facilitate a home school cooperative program. We have so many beautiful church buildings with great classroom space that are used one to three hours every week and sit empty the rest of the time. What a wonderful option to consider. I believe that God will call us to account for our stewardship of His church buildings.

It is our responsibility to teach the next generation of the blessings and faithfulness of God.

Walk about Zion, and go round about her: tell the towers thereof. Mark ye well her bulwarks, consider her palaces; that ye may tell it to the generation following. For this God is our God for ever and ever: he will be our guide even unto death. (Psalm 48:13)

The fifth thing that we can do is act. As the famous Patriot Pastor John Peter Gabriel Muhlenberg declared to his congregation in 1776, there is a time to pray and there is a time to fight and that time is now.

We have formed in our church "the Patrick Henry Club" that works under the authority of the pastor. An endless number of service opportunities are available through this club. Here are a few suggestions:

Monitor web sights like the American Family Association, Family Research Council, Focus on the Family, One News Now and other sources for REAL news that affects the morality of America and keeps members informed about attacks on

Christianity.

Provide Patrick Henry Alerts to be approved by your pastor and inserted in the bulletin. We need to be aware of legislation like the "Hate Crimes Bill" and let our representatives hear from us.

Prepare petitions on issues of importance to the Christian community, with the approval of your pastor, and set up a table in the foyer for those that wish to sign.

Monitor Patrick Henry Action Alerts sent out periodically through Reclaiming Oklahoma for Christ.

Provide materials and lesson plans to reestablish the truth of our Christian Heritage and the Role of Bible Believing Christians and Churches in America's History. Be educated on this subject so that you can teach classes or be available for public speaking in other churches, prayer breakfasts, or civic meetings.

Provide weekly "Moments of Truth" inserts to use in your church bulletins and local news papers and school papers.

Moment of Truth
From
Fairview Baptist Church

Thomas Jefferson, who supposedly is behind the misguided notion of Separation of Church and State, said this:

"God who gave us life gave us liberty. And can the liberties of a nation be thought secure when we have removed their only firm basis, a conviction in the minds of the people that these liberties are the Gift of God? That they are not to be violated but with his wrath? Indeed, I tremble for my country when I reflect that God is just; and His justice cannot sleep forever."

Fairview Baptist Church

1230 N. Sooner Rd. Edmond, OK
Corner of Sooner & Danforth 348-1745 Paul Blair - Pastor

Prepare for major events such as the annual "Rose Day" at the State Capitol. With a population of 3.5 million people in the State of Oklahoma, is it really unreasonable to think we could have 1% show up to lobby for the unborn?

Call and write letters to your elected representatives at all levels. Last year, while waiting to see one of my US Senators, I asked his receptionist a question, "How many phone calls do you get concerning an average bill?" I was expecting to hear a number in the hundreds; after all, this was a United States Senator. The answer was "about fifteen." Shocked, I further asked, "What if it's a real hot issue?" She said, "On a real hot button issue, we might get 60 calls." Don't think that your phone call or letter won't matter; it does. Think of the influence Christians could have on government policy at the national and local levels if even 25% of professing Christians let their voices be heard.

Write letters to families of those who have lost loved ones in Iraq or

Afghanistan. With each Oklahoman that gives his life, our church sends a letter with prayers and notes of encouragement from every member of the church who wishes to participate.

Send care packages to our soldiers. While we sleep in air-conditioned comfort and eat hot meals, many of our young men and women are living in harsh conditions in harm's way. Let us not forget them. Pray for them daily and send care packages and letters of encouragement and appreciation. Contact a local recruitment station and tell them what you would like to do. Last Christmas, we sent 100 packages containing snacks, toiletries and a Bible personally signed by one of our church members, along with notes written in crayon from our children's department. Those packages were welcome gifts received by 100 tired Marines.

Organize voter registration drives in your church. As citizens of the United States, Christians have the right to vote and must be registered. This is a legal right that can be performed within the local church.

Make voter guides available to your congregation. Groups in every state, like the Oklahoma Family Policy Council print non-partisan voter guides that report the facts about where each candidate stands on the issues. This also is a legitimate   non -biased, public service that can be performed within the church. We must be informed, as the scripture says in Proverbs 29:2, *"When the righteous are in authority, the people rejoice: but when the wicked beareth rule, the people mourn."*

These are just a few suggestions to start with, but there is no limit to the ways you may serve your community.

America was built on the backs of churches willing to stand for right in their day. Today, we have the same choice. We can either run from our culture or we can confront it and transform it through the power of the Holy Spirit.

If you are a member of a church that refuses to get involved, then perhaps you should find a church that will. As you read through the book of Acts, consider Paul's journeys. In every pagan city, he proclaimed the transforming Gospel of Jesus Christ. In every place, some believed, most didn't and usually a riot broke out. Should we be alarmed by the challenges we face today? May we as Christians be guilty of the charge that unbelievers laid against the church at Thessalonica, *"...these have turned the world upside down* (Acts 17:6)."

Chapter 9
Evil Triumphs When
Good Men Do Nothing

Every truth claim of God in the Holy Scriptures is absolutely true and will never fail.

One of the most obvious of these truth claim promises is found in Psalm 33:12, *"Blessed is the nation whose God is the LORD."*

Every empire built without acknowledging Almighty God, beginning with Nimrod's Babylon and ending with the Soviet Union, has crumbled into the ash heap of history. Why? *"Because blessed is the nation whose God is the LORD"* and, by inference, cursed is that nation whose god is not the LORD.

Is our land just more fertile than the other nations of the world? Are our oil reserves greater? Is our intellect and ingenuity far superior to that of others?   That is what the secularists want us to believe and that is exactly what God has warned us against.

"Beware that thou forget not the LORD thy God, in not keeping his commandments, and his judgments, and his statutes, which I command thee this day: Lest when thou hast eaten and art full, and hast built goodly houses, and dwelt therein; And when thy herds and thy flocks multiply, and thy silver and thy gold is multiplied, and all that thou hast is multiplied; Then thine heart be lifted up, and thou forget the LORD thy God... And thou say in thine heart, My power and the might of mine hand hath gotten me this wealth."
- Deuteronomy 8:11-17

America has lasted for 231 years because God is faithful to keep his conditional promise: *"Blessed is the nation whose God is the LORD."*

If God brought such fierce judgment upon the Nation of Israel for disobedience will He simply turn His head on the conduct of America?

I know that Jesus is coming again. It is written in the Book. I know that the devil winds up in the Lake of Fire. Hallelujah!! It is written in the Book.

But what if Jesus tarries for another ten years? What will America look like then? What if He tarries for twenty years or fifty? Will Christianity be against the law in Atheist America or Socialist America? Will we be governed by Sharia law? Will our children be forced to hide in the mountains and caves for their safety?

May we remember our heritage, return to Him, and be about His business until He comes again!!

"If my people, which are called by my name, shall humble themselves, and pray, and seek my face, and turn from their wicked ways; then will I hear from heaven, and will forgive their sin, and will heal their land."

2 Chronicles 7:14

With great appreciation for the knowledge received, learning at the feet of so many great Christian historians.

Resources for this book were compiled from the following:

My long time friend, historian and author Bill Federer and his collection of books including *America's God and Country* and *Backfired*.

My new friend, historian and author, the Rev. Peter Marshall and his collection of resources including *The Light and the Glory*.

The collection of work by the legendary historian of America's Christian Heritage, David Barton and *Wallbuilders*. The reading of his books, the accessing his website, and the first hand education received from a personal guided tour through the US Capitol.

The book *One Nation Under God* by David Gibbs and Jerry Newcombe.

The DVD *One Nation Under God* produced by Coral Ridge Ministries.

The King James Bible

The Library of Congress website

Printed in the United States
128854LV00002B/1/P

9 781606 432587